VOICE MESSAGE

T0080064

VOICE MESSAGE

KATHERINE BARRETT SWETT

AUTUMN
HOUSE PRESS

PITTSBURGH

"Autumn House Press" and "Autumn House" are registered trademarks owned by Autumn House Press, a nonprofit corporation whose mission is the publication and promotion of poetry and other fine literature.

 Autumn House Press receives state arts funding support through a grant from the Pennsylvania Council on the Arts, a state agency funded by the Commonwealth of Pennsylvania, and the National Endowment for the Arts, a federal agency.

Cover art: Johannes Vermeer, *Woman Holding a Balance*, 1664. Courtesy of the National Gallery of Art, Washington, D.C.
Text and cover design: Chiquita Babb

ISBN: 978-1-938769-52-8
Library of Congress Control Number: 2019949351

All Autumn House books are printed on acid-free paper and meet the international standards for permanent books intended for purchase by libraries.

CONTENTS

PART III   MARGINALIA

PART I

SONGS AND SONNETS

Grief brought to numbers cannot be so fierce,
For he tames it, that fetters it in verse.

—John Donne

CHAINSAW

One day it's gone, the tree outside, cut down
by selfish neighbors in the back who own
the square of pavement where the tree had grown
for decades; this ailanthus weed, self-sown,
provided moving shadows on the wall
and birdsong in the mornings as we woke.
It had already grown five stories tall,
a bit of wild in a concrete yoke.
Now every day we wake to what is wrecked—
the lonely silence of what's disappeared
and what remains: the pigeon's dreary coo
and knowing there is nothing we can do.
The citadels we thought were safe, sacked
and woods we thought forever woods, cleared.

TWO WOODCUTS

I Red Fuji

Sleeping daughter
in the next bed
I woke to red Fuji

every morning
wakes to my daughter
still dead

You should have woken me
she later said

Summer day Boston
Hokusai exhibit
Fuji blue and red

II Hiroshima Peace Memorial Park

Everywhere
in the park
light and peace

surround
a monumental grief
fierce not dark

the open wound
not the hard scar

paper around
floating fire

TWO VILLANELLES

I Flute Song

In every sound I hear, I see her lips
laughing or blowing in the silver flute.
The wind goes in and out until it stops.

And when she played, she gently swayed her hips
and kept time softly with her slippered foot.
In every single note, I hear her lips.

In every storm, I taste teardrops
and feel her stamp her leather boot.
The wind goes in and out until it stops.

And when she's mad, the gale force rips
the gutters off the streaming roof.
In every single blow, I feel her lips.

In every crack of every pear that drops,
she's always there among the bruised fruit.
The wind goes in and out until it stops;

it stops its tapping, tossing fingertips.
Let every voice and every song go mute.
In every sound I hear, I see her lips;
the wind goes in and out until it stops.

II Winter Light

I wish I could believe that ghosts were true
—a flashlight ready when the lights go out—
that death could leave behind a bit of you.

I pass you on the street; I interview
someone who tosses her black hair about.
I wish I could believe that ghosts were true.

Forget-me-nots return each year in blue;
your brother smiles and something in his mouth—
I think death left behind a bit of you.

I wear your yellow sweater from J. Crew
or hear a piece you practiced on the flute;
I can almost believe that ghosts are true.

The skin, the voice, the laugh, the *it* of you
grow daily more and more remote;
death's only left behind a bit of you,

which isn't you. The winter light comes through
your window on a thousand whirling motes.
I wish I could believe that ghosts were true
and death had left behind a bit of you.

THREE SONGS

I Father

Astronomers now all concur
that asteroids much prefer
smashing into Jupiter
than into any other.

His heavy-duty gravity
vacuums up calamity
and keeps the other planets free
from terrors temporarily.

II Never Disappear

Can you wait
for Queen Anne's lace,
black-eyed Susan's
orange face,
the meadow higher
than your knees,
heron fishing,
skunky breeze?

Can you wait
till autumn comes,
the pears are ripe,
chrysanthemums,
tomatoes hanging
from the vine,
jeans and sweaters
on the line?

Can you wait
for pale spring leaves,
for daffodils
and peonies?
Can you wait
another year
and maybe never
disappear?

III Song in Flood Time

All night we thought of tides
and winds and what they bring
and take and what survives.
We could not sing.

If we had stopped the flood
that covered everything
in salt and mud,
could we have sung?

If we had blocked the breeze
that made the church bells ring
and knocked down all the trees,
could we have sung?

Once when we climbed the hill
for water from the spring
we took our little fall;
then we could sing.

The sky above sinks deep into a lake.
Storefronts emerge from windows on a bus.
These double shots photographers all take
dissolve the distances that sever us.
The sunset pours out from the sliding glass;
a woman still inside holds out a tray.
A swimming pool is sprinkled with cut grass
and clouds the children scatter as they play.
Large monuments appear inside sunglasses;
green trees stand framed inside the fireplace,
a man glares through a windshield as he passes,
and in my pupils you see your drowned face,
and your brown eyes give my face back to me,
so mirrors make what can't be seem to be.

BRIGHT HAIR

. . . that this device might be some way

—John Donne

When you bury me, please place
our daughter's hair inside my fist;
that way some archaeologist,
who happens to unearth my grave,
might find this lock, not turned to gray
in all the intervening years
between my death and my daughter's.
I hope she'll be the kind to feel
the shock of immortality
I felt when sorting through old stuff
to find a hank of brown hair tied
some years before with bright red yarn
and curled up fetally inside
a Hellmann's mayonnaise jar.
I hope that scholar understands
just what my skeleton has in hand,
and finds the language to express
closer by that hair's breadth
that all we have are words and flesh.

SEVEN SONNETS

1 Yet Another View

It's terrifying to look down below
from thirty thousand feet and see the patches,
the crazy quilt that Midwest farmers sow
and farther north to see a great lake that matches
the lakes that lie on maps inside my head,
Ontario and Erie, Lake St. Clair,
somehow immediate, this distant spread,
although I've never actually walked down there.
What we have seen on maps seems to be there
as clichés often prove to be too true.
But it's no more accessible from air
than from the atlas on the bottom shelf,
and nothing saves you from the flat despair
that everything's a map except yourself.

II Voice Message

My brother's wife still answers when I call,
and he's not picking up. I say, "It's me.
Just saying hi, not anything at all."
I'm sure he senses my anxiety.
He picks up halfway through. "Hello. Hold on."
He turns it off. His voice is clear. He sounds
OK. He's there. Maybe he will hold on.
Amazing how the human soul rebounds.
I think her voice is like a rickety bridge
suspended there above a roaring creek
that rushes through a narrow mountain gorge.
Approaching grief is never for the meek.
She's gone. It's just my brother on the line
who seems to tell me, "Sure, I'm here. I'm fine."

III Missive

With every turn of phrase, I only drive
farther from her. A looming tree can seem
more real than she, its bare branches alive
to anyone who ever lived; indeed,
my words might conjure personality—
human type—some things are universal,
and anyone might sense mortality
touching the curling edges of a petal.
But she keeps slipping from my useless craft
circling the surface of the summer pond.
My line dangles. The bright fish uncaught
shivers away as leaves fall in the wind.
And yet I feel her with me every day
although to her there are no words, no way.

IV Stuff

Why do I have four typewriters secured
against calamities that I'll outlive
and have to write about? I'm pretty sure
that I'll be dead, but they will still survive
with no one left to write. I'm pretty sure
I have a rusty razor that once shaved
my father's face. I'm absolutely sure
I've stuff I long to toss that I once loved.
The worst part of the object fallacy
is trying to preserve you in what's left.
If I had none of it, none of this pelf
—old word good only for a rhyme, bereft
of quickening sense or easy intimacy—
would I remember better you, yourself?

V Summer Sonnet

A bullfrog calls across the pond at dusk
while children capture fireflies in jars.
As I rip off a dozen stiff corn husks,
a neighbor revs the engine of his car.
The bats keep swooping out in silent flight
and distant firecrackers cut the air.
We sit outside at dinner; it is light
till nine or ten, and we just linger there
because it seems like it will stay this way
always. We'll never change, never leave
this table here; these kids will always play
out there. Not one of us will grieve
a worse annoyance than the whine and bite
of bugs attacking on a summer night.

VI Penultimate

We always noted when the fish stopped leaping
or when we shoveled off the final snow;
we marked the date when tree frogs started peeping
or temperatures had reached their lowest low.
From those we calculated prior dates,
and time became like syllables of words,
as we searched out anti-penultimates
and what occurred before what then occurred.
We stopped the count, stopped finding fault
because we had to face our child's end.
We've felt no pride surviving an assault
that should have finished us, instead we tend
a future that somehow—somehow passed
the final syllable, to a new last.

VII City of Refuge

I dream we're exiled to a distant land,
a home for careless parents searching for
the lost, a place where locals understand
we'll never find what we had years before,
and when a stranger there makes idle chat,
we know he'll know that we have a dead child
or two and he does too and he'll know that
you talk about the dead as if alive.
For in the waking world we hesitate
to mention her; we have to make a choice
between our neighbor's staring at his plate
and somehow seeming to have lost his voice,
or our just saying that we have no daughter,
the way a drunk might say his gin was water.

PART II

VERMEER'S DAUGHTERS

Through painting, the faces of the dead go on living
for a very long time.

—Leon Battista Alberti

What parent knows the thoughts of a young daughter?
Assuming that his model was Maria,
Vermeer's first born, posed as he often caught her
giving that mocking look he used to see—a
kind I saw when my own teenage child
stared at me if I tried to interfere
with what she did; her challenges were mild,
a quiet distance captured by Vermeer.
And all the space around his characters
is calm, the open window, patterned tile.
The viewer's free to see what she prefers:
the suitor's leer, the maiden's too broad smile.
Some parents might be glad never to know
what her mysterious glance might really show.

What her mysterious glance might really show—
how can we guess? She doesn't look at us.
White letter floats above; blue dress below
spreads all around; her waist's voluminous
while flattened on the wall another globe
suggests the father writes from overseas.
But now the scholars say her ocean robe
may just be fashion and not pregnancy.
When I was pregnant I just looked too fat,
so on the bus most riders let me stand;
I'd read a book with half a mind on what
I read, another half on what I planned
or hoped to do once I had had my daughter,
a window opened on the sound of water.

A window opened on the sound of water,
her face is glowing with great happiness.
What is she thinking of, this burgher's daughter—
the beauty of her showy mustard dress,
his gallant gesture, confident and bold?
A velvet elbow in swashbuckling stance
creates a shining triangle of gold;
together they're an emblem of romance.
This memory of what love used to be—
a golden haze, a dash of velvet red,
a glass of wine, and possibility
of travel in the map above your head.
Now they're long gone and have nowhere to go;
Vermeer paints what we know we cannot know.

GIRL READING A LETTER
       AT AN OPEN WINDOW

Vermeer paints what we know we cannot know:
the light appears miraculously on pearls,
the figure vibrates in a yellow glow
that filters through the leaded pane. His girls
are either sinking deep inside their heads
or staring from the frame at Jan Vermeer
whose vision of their shining golden threads
the *camera* projected to his rear.
He paints another view of her that hovers,
a gibbous face faint in the window fog;
while scholars speculate about her lovers
and iconography they catalog—
the fallen fruit, the rumpled rug, gold curl—
I only feel the distance from the girl.

I only feel the distance from the girl
alone, asleep; we know our children drink
and in their drunkenness the room might whirl,
but we cannot imagine what they think.
X-rays show us an absent man, a dog
as if the work were painted by de Witte
(a pooch in church!) or Maes or Pieter de Hooch;
could she be drunk and snoring just a bit?
Above her on the wall, a painted mask
suggests that some small drama might exist,
but as I never got the chance to ask
whom my dead daughter might have loved or kissed
or if she died untouched—she never said—
before her is a solid barricade.

Before her is a solid barricade,
abandoned instruments and furniture,
a monument of light in stiff brocade,
a golden jacket trimmed in spotted fur
that signifies the season and the class
and that the painter liked this warmer hue
against her skin as she looks in the glass,
as if adornment's all she has in view.
She puts her mask on for the world to share,
the mask the painter paints and lets dissolve,
the mask that seems to say she does not care,
a mask whose studied beauty can't resolve
the meaning of this enigmatic girl,
a grace note struck that shimmers like a pearl.

A grace note struck that shimmers like a pearl,
the string her right hand casually picks,
as her left fingers elegantly curl
around the pegs; below, the harmonics
are sounding on the half-forgotten viol;
she's far from us, her back against the wall,
and does the curious glance, the subtle smile
suggest she hears her suitor in the hall?
No narrative's provided by Vermeer.
The lover might be far (the map behind);
the instrument might be a sign he's near.
I see in her something I need to find
but I can't hear the music that she made—
the image just the surface that she played.

The image just the surface that she played;
the music that the painter draws is not
more sweet than if the stops were pulled and stayed.
Like Orpheus, one sense is all we've got.
This caryatid holding up the sound
divides the painting as one might the strings
and splits the dark and light of the background,
so that it seems a perfect octave rings.
The music that he paints is so divine,
unwrapping all our tendons and our joints,
unstringing all the nerves along our spine;
it is not sound but light in brilliant points.
But still one sense is not enough for me;
her picture is a frail metonymy.

Her picture is a frail metonymy
of justice as the balance comes to rest;
behind her, Christ is sorting damned and free.
Pale as the damned, she weighs a nothingness.
Despite an urge I feel to simplify,
I can't clear out my daughter's childhood room,
to organize the clutter for the eye,
to leave the space wide open for the broom,
to narrow down my life to just one task,
to tune the instrument in morning's glare,
to be someone who never needs to ask,
to stand and stare but really not to care,
to feel myself become my social mask,
a single room that might be anywhere.

A single room that might be anywhere,
a black-edged frame contains the world for me:
a man, a window, instruments, a chair,
a glow that spreads inside just like the sea
whose briny smell came through to Jan Vermeer.
As if, at last, I'm in the lady's head,
as if her vision in my eyes appears:
fine wine, a globe, sheet music, letters, bread.
By emptying the room of extra stuff,
he underscores the overtones of space,
the countless symbols painted with a brush,
the outline of the loss we try to trace
when bodies sink into their gravity,
a plaster wall's the emptiness we see.

A plaster wall's the emptiness we see
behind the woman's strange reflected glow
when she's alone and she can finally
feel all the things she never wants to show:
familiar strands that follow endlessly,
the steady stitch that goes as it must go;
he paints the distance, strength, dexterity
behind the mundane tasks that women know.
The patience, art, and industry to sit
for hours dissolving in the sunny plaster,
a face half-lit, her fingers poised to knit,
and nothing telling her she must go faster.
In moments when our thoughts and work cohere,
we're every one of us a small Vermeer.

We're every one of us a small Vermeer,
our selves emerging from a hand or face.
This maid has massive shoulders, arms and rear
that fill and organize an emptied space.
The painter shows his own delight in work
by rendering her focus at her chore,
the elegant precision as she measures;
it seems the tiny tile at the floor
of Cupid might suggest some other pleasures.
The broken pane, the rough-hewn plaster textures
the wet-on-wet, impasto, glazes, scumbles,
techniques that scholars teach in schoolroom lectures,
the inward focus as the outward crumbles,
this knowledge that we're always on the brink
just as the liquid pours but never sinks.

YOUNG WOMAN WITH
       A WATER PITCHER

Just as the liquid pours but never sinks,
I every day defy the gravity,
deny there's any reason why I blink,
except perhaps a mote caught in my eye.
Behind her form, the map and sun-splotched walls,
the lightness where her dark dress is immured;
outside the colored glass, the morning calls
of sailors and the slap of boats secured.
Preparing her ablutions for the day,
she heard the neighbor's baby as she laughed,
and smelled the rotting food and salty spray;
she's shutting out the boats and morning draft—
but these are only my imagined links;
there is no story telling what she thinks.

There is no story telling what she thinks;
our own close-guarded children can't be known,
so we extrapolate from the small chinks
in adamantine armor they have grown.
Vermeer reminds me of my ignorance.
With any child, insight comes unplanned;
from time to time an unexpected glance
creates the image that we understand.
I try to find my daughter who is dead
in music, painting, or a carved stone name.
Her voice is gone, so many words unsaid,
a silent love the most we'll ever claim.
Outside the window there is sky and water.
What parent knows the thoughts of a young daughter?

What parent knows the thoughts of a young daughter,
what her mysterious glance might really show?
A window opened on the sound of water:
Vermeer paints what we know we cannot know.
I only feel the distance from the girl;
before her is a solid barricade,
a grace note struck that shimmers like a pearl,
the image just the surface that she played.
Her picture is a frail metonymy,
a single room that might be anywhere,
a plaster wall's the emptiness we see;
we're every one of us a small Vermeer,
just as the liquid pours but never sinks—
there is no story telling what she thinks.

PART III

MARGINALIA

In the marginalia, *too, we talk only to ourselves;
we therefore talk freshly—boldly—originally with*
abandonnement—*without conceit—*

—Edgar Allan Poe

MARGINALIA

I read my daughter's old Freud,
her college book, an introduction
to parapraxes, how we avoid

significance in small disruptions.
I read her margin notes,
quick summaries, and explanations

of his points. What's lost
is her. I want to hear her
make some crack to roast

the guy. I turn the page. Nearer:
she writes *Dad* by forgetting names,
and something makes her jot down *Flubber*.

I also look for hints of blame,
some scribbled clue about intent,
the words that might help me frame

the subsequent event.
Then this: *if worried about a slip—*
tend to—does that make it real? Or accident?

A friend said she stopped at the top.
We'll never know why she paused—
To catch the sun? Check out the slope?

Likely a patch of ice caused—
No way to know or to avoid—
She used to "why" and I'd "because,"
but now all answers are destroyed.

Constance Woolson died
in Venice, January 24—
an apparent suicide,
she was not yet 54.

Henry James said half one's feeling
for her was anxiety.
He wrote it repeatedly
in letters that scholars find revealing
of James's own anxiety.

He thought her cheerful manner a facade
as flowers set in the window
have nothing to do with what's inside.
Did he think how
the pots might fall below,
the careless maid knocking
them off the windowsill?
His metaphor is shocking
as Woolson was the pot that fell.

She would hate the bios and novels
about her lovelorn melancholy.
She was a writer who wanted readers,
and, of course, she was lonely,
living abroad, far from home, to save money.

I reread her novels most years.

I like the smell of old papers and books,
of library stacks, forgotten lives.

I take them like snuff in the afternoon,
the past boxed up like Bluebeard's wives.

Who isn't lonely as she grows older?

I clean the embossed spine
of *East Angels*, bought for nothing
when secondhand books first went online.
I spend hours dusting
and wiping each shelf with lavender oil
to fight off mildew and soil.

The last Christmas she turned down
all invitations. She wanted to be alone
with her things and memories.
Her gondola wound
for miles around the lagoon.

I am now her age, and I don't believe
she killed herself for love.
Hers was a deeper grief,
and she was not afraid to die;
she wrote that repeatedly.

James couldn't get over
that suicide is impolite
—it seemed so out of character—
like refusing to eat your host's meat.
I think she reached the limit
of memory, writing, and stuff.
Even a gentle lady has the right
to say enough, not enough, enough.

The country has abandoned it,
    but not the wild.
        Crack addicts sit

on ruined benches in the park,
    crows call from plane
        trees, pit bulls bark

at children playing in the glass,
    the dirtied dream
    of bureaucrats

who hoped once to commemorate
    local genius,
    not recreate

the House of Usher, death, unrest,
    delirium.
        Our guide confessed,

"I sleep in the house when I can.
    I have a room
        in Manhattan,

but it's quiet here and near Fordham
    where I'm in school.
        At four a.m.

I even play my violin.
    No one complains."
        We followed him,

stooping as we came inside
　　　the dark, low walls
　　　　　where his child bride

lay in a room three paces wide,
　　　only a coat and cat
　　　　　for warmth, and died.

THE SUN RISING

Busy old fool

—John Donne

While all across the town they're waking up
to curse the clock and make their morning tea,
to rouse the kids or walk the restless pup,
and look back at their bedrooms longingly,
I think the sun's fantastic, rising up
and pouring in with youthful, yellow gleam
and squeezing orange in my reddish cup
and slipping in the curtains as I dream.
Old fools, we're lying in the bed we made,
for nothing else is calling to us now;
escaping summer's heat in oaken shade,
a lazy bull and even lazier cow,
we, unlike those young fools, now realize
that one day our sun will, in fact, not rise.

ARTIFICIAL NIGHTINGALE

I think I heard a nightingale inside
the olive grove, but do they sing in the day?
I do not know. I only know he cried
the way the artificial one I played
would chirp repeatedly until I wound
the pin too tight and broke the fragile thing,
a nineteenth-century folly someone found,
concocted of some feathers and a spring.
I think it was a nightingale I heard
and not at all mechanical. I found
the imitation one had been absurd,
a faint cartoon of nature's fuller sound,
but even this just brought me to the brink
of hearing a true nightingale, I think.

Stuck in that small, sleepy town
where the wind blows the dust in most days
and the neighbor's cow tramples down
the frail lettuces, she flays
the trees with her tongue as she strips
a chicken of feathers and, sweating, dismembers
its limbs. Glimpsing her man as he slips
out the gate with his grin and gun, she remembers
how once his hard hips hooked above her thighs,
his odd twitch and gasp as she pulled him in
to her own triumph caught in his widening eyes.
Those lines that use has pulled so thin
she still tries to knot with rage to flog
his impotence, his affection for the dog.

DON GIOVANNI

I've reached the age when finally I'm sure
that I could take the Don for a quick ride—
a menopausal female body tour
of every wrinkle out and some inside.
I've finally put my Mad Elvira down,
at what steep cost no man will ever know,
but Don Giovanni knows his way around
the body and I'm ready for a go.
Pure lust at my ripe age, one night in bed,
and in the morning, little or nothing said,
put on my clothes without a second thought;
love is something borrowed now, not bought.
And yet to make my pleasure quite complete
I'd want to throw him begging in the street.

GERTRUDE STEIN

Do you see it look like that?
—Stein on Juan Gris

Gertrude Stein walks on a sentence
and it breaks in two. On a fence
her great bulk balances lightly.
Some find her, her syntax unsightly;
her spliced ungainly phrases
experiments and compromises.
I love how prepositions verb
and nouns worn as adverbs disturb
the peace of the neighbors
who rest on the rest of their labors.
Gertrude Stein had good neighbors
and was one, rest assured.
No one, not a board, was bored.

HELEN AT THE DISTAFF

*She slipped a drug that had the power of robbing grief
and anger of their sting*

—Homer

From him there's no reproach; it is enough
to get her back again, to hold her thighs,
to see his gray beard in her open eyes.
The heavy distaff drops and draws yarn off,
a slender wrist jerks from the wide cuff.
And glancing at her tapestry, she sighs.
It needs more color, yellows, bolder dyes.
She picks up clumps of wool and feels their rough
texture. Why spin it very tight? She smooths
her woolen robe. He says he likes her face
aging to godly repose. She can't erase
the outline of the burning walls, the oaths
of men who hate her still. But there are drugs—
she can weave the truth into her rugs.

PENELOPE AND THE SUITORS

Wasn't there one she thought of lying with
as she unraveled rows of grass and flowers
and wondered what she might be buying with
this trick, years after he destroyed Troy's towers?
Wasn't there one for whom she could cast off
the years of loneliness, one never named
whose clumsy ways and accent made her laugh,
who glanced at her so shyly as he gamed?
A young son left no privacy but dreams,
which nightly whispered neither lies nor truth:
her husband holds a goddess in his arms
while suitors stare at her and rob her farms;
she drags him matted, briny, safe from harms
and squeezes ghosts of women from his mouth.

FAIRY TALE

The youngest child is left at home alone
with parents tired of the endless years
of making do, pursuing their careers,
spending too much time on their cell phones,
and finding causes for their aching bones.
Suddenly, this gorgeous youth appears
who should be wearing armor, crossing spears
with dwarves and giants, trolls and evil crones.
He's not, in fact, a changeling, as he seems,
but just an adolescent still at home
as restless as a foundling prince who dreams
of fleeing from the fisherman's poor shack
and sweeping through the fields to fight what comes
knowing that once he leaves, he won't be back.

STORAGE

He puts away sports trophies, childish things,
throws out the Simpson doll he loved at twelve,
clears out some space for new books on the shelves,
the Sartre next to *The Fellowship of the Ring,*
The Brothers K, Das Capital, The Wings
of the Dove—how quickly adolescence delves
into the multiplicity of selves
that sixteen years in one small bedroom bring.
A bit of Lego buried in the rug's
worn pile reminds me of the eight-year-old,
happy to talk, so casual with hugs;
his voice was high and shoulders not so broad.
And now that younger boy is safely stored
inside the one whose look can stop me cold.

WINE

Two things I can still manage / wine and poetry

—Tu Fu

Fine food is not the reason I love wine;
it's love for singing in a tone-deaf world,
for sudden liquidness in legs and spine,
dancing like thin spaghetti slowly twirled
around a fork while drunken men expound
on metaphysics launched into thin air,
weak arguments that soon crash to the ground,
but I'm so high I really couldn't care.
All judgment and some memories are drowned,
for when we drink, we drink with those we see
to those we loved, to those who aren't around,
to summers past spent swimming in the sea,
to children's backs warm to the touch and browned
as if with wine we drink up memory.

I read you some translations by Tu Fu,
as all around tree shadows on the lawn
sparkle with the flashy multitude
of fireflies that show up every June.
The government decays, but they appear,
a disco frenzy stretching to the sky,
above our heads, below, in front, to the rear,
impossible to trace with just the eye.
The night comes late, the air feels warm and wet;
our dinner's done, but it is good to drink
with bats, bullfrogs, pond moon; good to forget
how many states we've seen rise up and sink,
how many summers we've seen disappear
and wondered if we'd see what comes next year.

VOICE MESSAGE

IN GRATITUDE

So many people have contributed to this book. That I could write at all is because of you.

Thank you to the team at Autumn House Press for making the publication process so easy: Christine Stroud, Chiquita Babb, Mike Good. Thank you to Erica Dawson for choosing my manuscript for the Donald Justice Poetry Prize, and to Jesse Waters, Luke Stromberg, and Cyndy Pilla at West Chester University Poetry Center for organizing such a spectacular conference. Thank you to the family of Iris M. Spencer who endow the Donald Justice Poetry Prize.

Thank you to my inspiring teacher, Marie Ponsot, who died too soon to see this book in print, and to all my poet friends: Laura Ciraolo, Emily Fragos, Scott Hightower, Julie Kane, Jee Leong Koh, Thomas March, Patricia Markert, Emily McKeague, L.B. Thompson, Jamie Stern, Andrew Sunshine, Marjorie Tesser, Clyde Tressler, Catherine Woodard, Cynthia Zarin. I am grateful for so many years of meetings, workshops, and readings around New York.

Thank you to the administration at the Brearley School, particularly James Mulkin and Jane Fried, for providing me with the sabbatical leave in 2016–2017 during which many of these poems were written.

Thank you to all my colleagues at the Brearley School who have made coming to work a joy, in particular those in the English department: Renate, Tara, Sherri, Susan, Heyden, Helaine, Caroline, Olivia, and Cordelia. Your brilliance has made me think in new ways about literature and writing.

Thank you to my students for being so willing to read and to write poetry.

Thank you to my lifelong friends: Martine, Derrick, Nenna, Alastair, Anne, Claire, Chris, Clare, Mark, Rebecca, George, Fredrika, Matthew, Jane, Alexandra, Joni, Michel, Nick, Lisa, Randy, Joe, Morgen, Margie, Monique, Will, Emily, Alex, Geirþrúður.

Thank you to my large and loving family, my sisters and brother, my mother and in-laws, my cousins and aunts.

Thank you to my dear sons, Nicky and Willie. You make me proud; you make me think; you make me laugh.

Finally, thank you to my beloved Benjy, who reads every word I write with enthusiasm and a pencil. I am lucky to love and be loved. This book is dedicated to him.

In memory of Martha, Marvin, Rachel, Julie, and Elizabeth.

ACKNOWLEDGMENTS

These poems appeared, sometimes in slightly different form, in the following publications.

The Lyric Magazine: "Father" and "Late This Summer Night"

Measure: "Yet Another View" (Finalist 2016 Howard Nemerov Sonnet Award) and "Summer Sonnet" (Finalist 2017 Howard Nemerov Sonnet Award)

Mezzo Cammin: "Gertrude Stein," "Helen at the Distaff," "Penelope and the Suitors," "Penultimate," "Stuff," "Fairy Tale," "Storage," and "Vermeer's Daughters"

Nasty Women Poets: An Unapologetic Anthology of Subversive Verse: "Don Giovanni"

The Orchards Poetry Journal: "Artificial Nightingale" and "The Sun Rising"

The Raintown Review: "Voice Message"

Rattle: "The Poe Cottage, 1992"; "Dust"; "Marginalia"; and "City of Refuge"

The Road Not Taken: "Winter Light"

Still Against War: Poems for Marie Ponsot (I-VIII): "Song in Flood Time," "Missive," "Mrs. Van Winkle," "Two Villanelles," "Chainsaw," and "What Can't Be"

A high school English teacher, Katherine Barrett Swett lives in New York City. She received a PhD in American Literature from Columbia University. Her poems have been published in various journals, including *The Lyric Magazine*, *Rattle*, *Mezzo Cammin*, *The Raintown Review*, and *The Orchards*. Her sonnets were finalists for the Nemerov Contest in 2016 and 2017. Her chapbook, *Twenty-One*, was published by Finishing Line Press in 2016.

NEW AND FORTHCOMING RELEASES

Heartland Calamitous by Michael Credico

Voice Message by Katherine Barrett Swett ◆ Winner of the 2019
Donald Justice Poetry Prize, selected by Erica Dawson

The Gutter Spread Guide to Prayer by Eric Tran ◆ Winner of the 2019
Rising Writer Prize, selected by Stacey Waite

Praise Song for My Children: New and Selected Poems by Patricia Jabbeh Wesley

under the aegis of a winged mind by makalani bandele ◆ Winner of the 2019
Autumn House Poetry Prize, selected by Cornelius Eady

Hallelujah Station by M. Randal O'Wain

Grimoire by Cherene Sherrard

Further News of Defeat: Stories by Michael X. Wang ◆ Winner of the 2019
Autumn House Fiction Prize, selected by Aimee Bender

Skull Cathedral: A Vestigial Anatomy by Melissa Wiley ◆ Winner of the 2019
Autumn House Nonfiction Prize, selected by Paul Lisicky

For our full catalog please visit: http//www.autumnhouse.org